This book belongs to

_____

I
AM
LOVE

YOU ARE LOVE

by Lauren Tatner

illustrated by Angelina Doherty

Copyright © 2022 Lauren Tatner

All rights reserved. No part of this book may be used or reproduced by any means, graphic, electronic, or mechanical, including photocopying, recording, taping or by any information storage retrieval system without the written permission of the publisher, except in the case of brief quotations embodied in critical articles and reviews.

ISBN: 978-1-7780585-0-9 (print)
ISBN: 978-1-7780585-1-6 (ebook)

Legal deposit – Bibliothèque et Archives nationales du Québec, 2022.
Legal deposit – Library and Archives Canada, 2022.

Editor/Consultant: Ruthie Klein, BSW
Illustrator/Graphic Designer: Angelina Doherty
Author photo: Brad Tatner

Published by Law of Happy, Montreal, Quebec, Canada

www.lawofhappy.com

This book is dedicated with love to
Hannah, Evalee, Starbie

And to You
Always remember, You Are Love

Introduction

You Are Love is an illustrated and interactive love-centered guide to happiness for adults and children.

Babies come into this world knowing that life is supposed to be fun and that anything is possible. They are great teachers of life. They are quick to smile, to laugh freely, and to be in the moment. Sadly, as they are growing up, what they intuitively knew as babies becomes replaced with learned self-limiting beliefs. And then, endlessly, they search outside of themselves for happiness.

This book's message is a reminder of what you were born knowing, and what children and your inner child want you to remember —

- ❤ Your happiness comes from within
- ❤ You have your own internal guidance system (your emotions)
- 💛 You are special just as you are
- 💚 Your natural state is one of well-being
- 💙 You have the ability to create anything you want
- 💙 Your main purpose in life is to have fun
- 💜 You are energy at your core and that energy is Love

As you read or sing [as I do] through the book, do you notice each of the seven colors of the rainbow? Each rainbow color has its own special beauty.

Then have fun with the interactive portions on the illustrated pages. It further inspires inner dialogue, open conversation, and emotional connection.

And look out for a feather within the illustrations. I believe that when you find a feather, it's a sign from your angels that you are never alone.

May this book awaken and nourish your radiant inner child. May it encourage children to trust all they were born knowing. May we be playful and kind as we practice together.

Always Love,

Lauren

I feel love when I _____

You are Love
and
You are Loved

I have fun when I ───────

You create your own happiness
In a special way
You choose
Thoughts that feel good to you
You
laugh, sing, dance, **and** play

my inner strengths (super powers) are _____

You trust
You have everything
You need
Inside of you

Look within
See how *you feel*
Your emotions and inner wisdom
Will guide you through

It feels good to know
That what you
Think
    Feel
Say
  and
Do
    is...

**Special
Unique
Because there's just
One of YOU**

It's fun to imagine (or daydream about) _____

Love, Well-Being
Happiness and Peace
All good things flow
imagine
    believe
        then
           see

Describe your peaceful place, what's it like?
(I see _____, I hear _____, I smell _____, I feel _____)

Your part
Is to allow
Relax
Feel Good
And just BE!

All that you want
To be, do, or have
Is yours
To create for fun

I appreciate ―――――

You celebrate
You appreciate
Each moment
Each year
Around the sun

I love when we ―――

Thank you
For being you
and
For choosing me

I have fun when I play

I love
To see you
Play and grow
And that we trust
All is well
Yippee!

I am loved even when I ———————

You're an eternal being
I love you as you are
A bright and beautiful soul

I know that _____
(choose affirmation below or create your own)

Self-Love
Is a practice
So be kind
Smile
You are
Human
and
Whole!

Acknowledgments

My deep appreciation to my twins for inspiring the writing of this book. When you were born, your loving energy and presence brought me back to what I was born knowing, and the words flowed through me onto the pages. Thank you for being you and for choosing me. I love you.

Thank you to my late grandparents, Harry and Eva Klein, for whom my twins are lovingly named. As survivors of the Holocaust, who rebuilt their lives in Canada, thank you for teaching me about believing, visualizing, valuing oneself, love, kindness, resilience, and appreciating life's simple pleasures. These principles form the basis of my book.

Thank you to Esther Hicks (and Abraham and Jerry), John Kobel, Dr. Brian Weiss, Mom, Dad, Jon, Sari, Brad, Starbie, and to everyone who has and who continues to inspire me along the way.

Biography

Lauren Tatner, founder of Law of Happy, is an inspirational teacher and speaker. A bilingual native Montrealer, Lauren is a graduate of Université de Montréal, Faculty of Law, where she earned four law degrees.

Lauren is certified as a Reiki Teacher, Consulting Hypnotist and Meditation Teacher, Laughter Yoga Leader, and Fitness Instructor Specialist. She also trained in Theatre, Dance, Zumba, Voice, Mediation, Public Speaking, Improv, Clown, Comedy, Past Life Regression (with American Psychiatrist, Dr. Brian Weiss, and Carole Weiss), Shamanism, and Qigong.

Lauren has always been fascinated with the mind, body, and spirit connection. She is passionate about teaching the power of laughter, meditation, and movement in a fun and relatable way. When Lauren gives talks and leads workshops in the corporate and private sectors, she uses a unique approach that integrates elements of her diverse skills and experience.

Lauren is the mother of twins and a rescue pup. You can visit her at www.lawofhappy.com

YOU ARE LOVE

is also available in French

ISBN: 978-1-7780585-2-3 (print - French)
ISBN: 978-1-7780585-3-0 (ebook - French)

www.ingramcontent.com/pod-product-compliance
Lightning Source LLC
Chambersburg PA
CBHW040159100526
44590CB00001B/14